POET SAFARI

Verses From England

Edited By Warren Arthur

25 Years of YoungWriters

First published in Great Britain in 2017 by:

YoungWriters
Est. 1991

Young Writers
Remus House
Coltsfoot Drive
Peterborough
PE2 9BF
Telephone: 01733 890066
Website: www.youngwriters.co.uk

All Rights Reserved
Book Design by Spencer Hart
© Copyright Contributors 2017
SB ISBN 978-1-78820-464-4
Printed and bound in the UK by BookPrintingUK
Website: www.bookprintinguk.com
YB0333BY

Foreword

Dear Reader,

Welcome to this book packed full of feathery, furry and scaly friends!

Young Writers' Poetry Safari competition was specifically designed for 5-7 year-olds as a fun introduction to poetry and as a way to think about the world of animals. They could write about pets, exotic animals, dinosaurs and you'll even find a few crazy creatures that have never been seen before! From this starting point, the poems could be as simple or as elaborate as the writer wanted, using imagination and descriptive language.

Given the young age of the entrants, we have tried to include as many poems as possible. Here at Young Writers we believe that seeing their work in print will inspire a love of reading and writing and give these young poets the confidence to develop their skills in the future. Poetry is a wonderful way to introduce young children to the idea of rhyme and rhythm and helps learning and development of communication, language and literacy skills.

These young poets have used their creative writing abilities, sentence structure skills, thoughtful vocabulary and most importantly, their imaginations, to make their poems and the animals within them come alive. I hope you enjoy reading them as much as we have.

Warren Arthur

Contents

Friars Academy, Wellingborough

Lily Rose Weatherhead (12)	1
Tyler West (12)	2

Great Creaton Primary School, Creaton

Isabella Monich (5)	3
Ellis (5)	4
Rory (5)	5
JJ Eldred (5)	6
Christian Reger (6)	7
Sam Eldred (7)	8
Alfie Barron Leah (6)	9
Arabella (5)	10
Zala Leskovsek (5)	11

Heckington St Andrew's CE School, Heckington

Nicola Motyka (4)	12
Joshua Ray Carl Thompson (5)	13
Viktorija Urbaite (6)	14
Logan Bentley (7)	15
Anastasia Corbould (5)	16

Horning Community Primary School, Horning

Grace Scott (6)	17
Karlis Bontis (7)	18
Charlie Marsden (6)	19
Freddie Hardingham (6)	20

Marshchapel Primary School, Marshchapel

Grace-Olivia Wheatley (7)	21

Sidegate Primary School, Ipswich

Molly Allen (6)	22
Alex Townes (7)	24
George Ribbans (7)	26
Connor Ditcham (7)	27
Aiden Hughes (7)	28
Amber Kaur Birak (7)	29
Ananya Pravin Desai (7)	30
Freddie Moy (7)	31
Darcey Oakes (7)	32
Lewis Rowland (7)	33
Attila Tanase (6)	34
Madelyn Ashford (7)	35
Layla Moreno-Roberts (7)	36
Reyah Amber Haayat (7)	37
Amalia Tutu (7)	38
Eban Bird (7)	39
Lacey Mae Wedlow (6)	40
Lexi Thaine (7)	41
Joseph Freezer (7)	42
Scarlett Burrows (7)	43
Olivia Ferjani (7)	44
Jessica Danielle Riley (7)	45
Bethany Bugg (7)	46
Zuzanna Parcinska (7)	47
Riley Emberson (7)	48
Miles William O'Keefe (7)	49
Autumn Lily Oakes (7)	50
Yasmin Fermor (6)	51
Bailey Miller (6)	52

Arthur Barnes (7)	53
Phoebe-Mae Garrard (7)	54
Grace Markham (7)	55
Rieshy Mahadevan Ramesh (7)	56

St George's Primary & Nursery School, Great Yarmouth

Yury Vieira (6)	57
Philip James Edwards (7)	58
Cory Cook (6)	59
Matas Gelumbeckas (7)	60

St John's Community Primary School & Nursery, Hoveton

Ellicia Soglo (6)	61
Mia Coxall (6)	62
Hunter Lucas (5)	63
Barnaby Hurren (6)	64

St Joseph's Catholic Primary School, Derby

Daniel Milton (11)	65

St Oswald's CE Primary School, Ashbourne

Issey Breeze	66
Sebastian Tinsley (6)	67
Maisie Kerr (7)	68
Franek Lasek (6)	69
Jess Wilson (7)	70
Noah Wood (7)	71
Josie Leslie (7)	72
Macy Grocott (7)	73

Stanground St John's Academy, Stanground

Laura Tozer (6)	74
Evie Rose Peacock (6)	75
Joáo Davi Gutierrez Da Silva (5)	76
Laura Majcher (6)	77

Laylah Jayne Louise Jago (6)	78
Tia Fitzpatrick (7)	79
Cherry Rae Coy (6)	80
Jaiden Walton (6)	81
Victor DJu (6)	82
Kacey Wharton (6)	83
Ben Dale McBean (5)	84
Nancy Tasker (6)	85
James Owen Ady Lanning (6)	86
Aleksandra Detka (6)	87
Tyler Maughan (6)	88

Ten Mile Bank Riverside Academy, Ten Mile Bank

Anya Rai Rendle (7)	89
Tianna Louise Brassett (6)	90
Caroline Amanda Rolph (6)	91
Ella Mae Brassett (7)	92
Annabelle Coogan (6)	93
Angel Langley (7)	94

The Gainsborough Parish Church Primary School, Gainsborough

Grace Hills (7)	95
William Thompson (7)	96
Holly-Anne Marie Bew (7)	97
Lukus Hurst (6)	98
Mylee Tuplin (6)	99
Harry Snell (6)	100
Finley Thorold (7)	101
Scarlett Louise Duffield (6)	102
Emily Louise Ashby (6)	103
Taya Beckett (7)	104
Mia Rose Purvis (6)	105
Elliot Taylor (7)	106
Fern Jefferson (7)	107
Henry Corfield (7)	108
Yasmin Joy Clarkson (7)	109
Brooke Chapman (7)	110
Ryan John Anderson (6)	111
Blake Palmer (6)	112
Levi Coombe (7)	113

Tayla-Mae Gray (6)	114
Maisie Pulford (7)	115
Amber Currie (6)	116
Finley Wilson (7)	117
Erica Fairless (6)	118
Katie Rose Birkitt (7)	119
Reuben Cave (6)	120
Sophie Burnett (6)	121
Amber Brewer (7)	122
Maddison Merrills (6)	123
Keela Galloway (7)	124
Logan Dre Woodrow (6)	125
Freya Mawer (7)	126
Joel Waller (5)	127
Laura Moutinho (7)	128
Ellie Drayton (6)	129
Tobey Hallam (6)	130
Kristie Denniss (7)	131
Courtney Anna Gloria Turner (6)	132
Harry James Townsend (7)	133
Kacie-Jo White (6)	134
Leah Potts (5)	135
Liam Levick (7)	136
Maisie Grace Swinton (6)	137
Maximiliaan Kwant (6)	138
Corey Simons (6)	139
Oonagh Stark (6)	140
Hanna Corringham (5)	141
Declan McConnell (6)	142
Alex Jennings (5)	143
Noah Stobbs (6)	144
Phoebe-Louise Garnham (6)	145

Westhouses Primary School, Westhouses

Layla Kerry Smith (7)	146
Liam Lowe (7)	148
Mason Greaves (6)	149
Joseph David Morton (6)	150
Emmi (7)	151
Olivia Wilson (6)	152
Paiton Toseland (7)	153

The Poems

The Trip

Mia and Cat went to play in the rain
and then they went on a train.
On the train they played I Spy.
Mia lost so she started to cry.
The train slowed down,
they got off at the stop
so they went to the shop,
then they went on a ride
and then they went to hide.

Lily Rose Weatherhead (12)
Friars Academy, Wellingborough

How A Dragon Behaves

D ragon likes to eat
R ats, roast chicken, rubbish
A nd, really annoying people.
G irls are annoying for Dragon.
O range is Dragon's favourite colour.
N aughty Dragon breathes fire at people.

Tyler West (12)
Friars Academy, Wellingborough

What Am I?

I have four legs, black spots
And sharp teeth.
I am faster than a red car
But slower than a cheetah.
I have claws as sharp as knives.
I can hide between the trees.
I look very cute,
But you wouldn't want me as a pet!
My favourite food is antelope.
What am I?

A jaguar.

Isabella Monich (5)
Great Creaton Primary School, Creaton

What Am I?

I have four legs, two eyes
And soft fur.
I am faster than a racing car
But slower than a jet.
I have teeth as sharp as knives.
I like to hide between two trees.
I am very fierce
And roar very loudly.
I am the king of the jungle.
What am I?

A lion.

Ellis (5)
Great Creaton Primary School, Creaton

What Am I?

I was once dead.
I am slower than a jet
But faster than a dog.
I have eyes as bright as car headlights.
I like to hide in the grass.
I am a cross between a lion's back
And a zebra's front.
What am I?

A quagga.

Rory (5)
Great Creaton Primary School, Creaton

What Am I?

I have no legs,
Two eyes and a long tongue.
I am longer than a worm
But shorter than a train.
I have teeth as sharp as knives.
I like to curl up in a tree.
I like to squeeze you very tightly.
I hiss through the trees.
What am I?

JJ Eldred (5)
Great Creaton Primary School, Creaton

What Am I?

I am dangerous.
I am smaller than a car
But bigger than a twig.
My teeth are like a sharp knife.
I live under the lake.
I have a long tail with spikes on.
I go *snap!*
What am I?

A crocodile.

Christian Reger (6)
Great Creaton Primary School, Creaton

What Am I?

I am fierce.
I am slower than a cheetah
But faster than a cricket.
My nose is like a pointy arrow.
I keep my eyes above the water.
I have a scaly back
And I go *snap!*
What am I?

A crocodile.

Sam Eldred (7)
Great Creaton Primary School, Creaton

What Am I?

I live in Africa.
I am noisier than a man,
But quieter than a lion.
My teeth are as sharp as a knife.
I sleep on a damp tree.
I am black.
I am a type of cat.
What am I?

A black panther.

Alfie Barron Leah (6)
Great Creaton Primary School, Creaton

What Am I?

I live in Africa.
I am quieter than a parrot
But noisier than a mouse.
I am as fluffy as a teddy bear.
I like to hide behind trees.
I am like a deer.
What am I?

A dik-dik.

Arabella (5)
Great Creaton Primary School, Creaton

What Am I?

I can be angry.
I am bigger than a mouse
But smaller than an elephant.
I am as long as a hosepipe
I slither down a tree.
What am I?

A snake.

Zala Leskovsek (5)
Great Creaton Primary School, Creaton

Raa-Raa The Noisy Lion!

In safari jungle it is a nice, quiet morning
But then someone
With a big noise wakes up everyone.
Of course that is Raa-Raa, the noisy lion.
Raa-Raa wants to play hide-and-seek.
Friends agree to play that game.
The lion turns to hide.
Lion hides deep in the bush
But then felt tired and fell asleep.
Friends could not find the lion
But then from a nearby bush
They heard a strange sound.
There was a snoring, tired lion.

Nicola Motyka (4)
Heckington St Andrew's CE School, Heckington

The Hunting Dino-Pig

My best friend is a flying dino-pig.
He glows in the dark and is green and big.
He lives on a fire farm
And chases guinea pigs into the barn.
He plays funny football
And eats screaming girls
Which is not cool.
He flies up high
And sounds like a snapping crocodile
And when he comes back down
It takes him a while.
He smells like a mouldy pig
But after all, he is my best friend
And his head is big.

Joshua Ray Carl Thompson (5)
Heckington St Andrew's CE School, Heckington

Flamingo's Life

On a left leg or the right,
The flamingos have arrived,
They are nice, pinky light
And can fly very high.
They like to stay in the water
Where it's hot,
They stand on one leg,
On the spot.
They like to eat smelly fish
But not stingy jellyfish.

Viktorija Urbaite (6)
Heckington St Andrew's CE School, Heckington

My Puppy

Franklin looks like a cute baby dinosaur.
He is fast like a raptor and a T-rex.
He sleeps like a tiger and a lion would.
He is a beautiful puppy
And his room looks like a calm place.
I love my dog!

Logan Bentley (7)
Heckington St Andrew's CE School, Heckington

Fluffy, Hop, Hop

I have a pet
She lives in a hutch
She munches on carrots
I love her so much
She is my very good pet.

Anastasia Corbould (5)
Heckington St Andrew's CE School, Heckington

The Lion

The lion can roar all the way to Wroxham.
Roarrrrr!
His fur is like a marshmallow.
He is from the cat family.
He can jump really high.
He likes shade.
He is as fluffy as a bottom.

Grace Scott (6)
Horning Community Primary School, Horning

The Lion

Roar like a T-rex.
Fiery tail like lava.
Poisoned teeth like bows and arrows.
Claws like swords.
He has got a black medal.
He has a golden hat.

Karlis Bontis (7)
Horning Community Primary School, Horning

The Lion

His tail is like a pickaxe.
Humps and stripes.
Mane like flames.
Roar like a thunder strike.

Charlie Marsden (6)
Horning Community Primary School, Horning

The Lion

Hair like coal
Tail like string
Eyes like zeros
Claws like horns.

Freddie Hardingham (6)
Horning Community Primary School, Horning

Kyle The Koala!

Up in the tall trees
Lives something grey and fluffy.
His name is Kyle.
He has a lovely smile.
Kyle climbs up very high
And wishes he could fly
But koalas don't have wings.
Oh he really is a funny thing.
He likes to play with his friends
And he drives his mum around the bend.

Grace-Olivia Wheatley (7)
Marshchapel Primary School, Marshchapel

The Superhero

Once upon a time there was a dog
who slept and slept.
His friends thought, *mmm,*
maybe we should do something
for his birthday.
'We should take him to the funfair.
Let's get him out so he can have some fun.'
But when they tried
they couldn't get him out.
It was so hard.
When they said funfair he ran out the door
and screamed, 'Let's go!'
They went but it was so wet
they couldn't go on any rides.
They were so wet
but when they went into the car park
there was a problem.
Chris went right up and said, 'Don't worry,

I will save you!'
He did not know what he was doing
but then he yawned fire breath.
He did not know how he did it.
Ever since everyone has been asking,
'Do your super power!'
He knew who had given him
the superpower
so he went to talk to him.
He said, only if he would run on a machine
That made him look like he was chicken.
So after, he took away his superpowers
so he did only one more thing.
He told everyone
he didn't have superpowers.
And after that everyone
went back to normal.

Molly Allen (6)
Sidegate Primary School, Ipswich

The Strange Cat Dentist

The cuddly cat pushes the red button.
The chair slowly rises then descends.
The bearded man opens his mouth
and says, 'Argh!'
Suddenly the cat's tummy starts to rumble
like a giant volcano about to erupt.
The sleeves of his uniform start to split.
His claws ascend upwards like giant swords.
The pupils in his eyes of coal
start to flame red.
Buttons pop off
when his body grows gigantic.
His small teeth start to grow
into enormous great fangs.
Drool slips from his mouth
and slides down his hairy body.

Quickly, he gobbles the bearded man up
and turns to his normal self again.
'Mmm! That was yummy!' he says.

Alex Townes (7)
Sidegate Primary School, Ipswich

Lily The Cat-Hen

Lily the cat-hen looked different.
No other animal is the same.
Her head is a cat and her body a chicken,
She really looks rather strange!

She sleeps under my bed at night-time,
Keeping the neighbours awake.
The only way to shut her up
Is to feed her birthday cake!

Every time she sees the cake
She runs like an alligator to eat it.
I have to be quick to feed her,
Or my fingers will end up being bit!

She may be strange and different,
But I love her just the same.
Lily the cat-hen, my best friend,
Nobody else fits the frame!

George Ribbans (7)
Sidegate Primary School, Ipswich

My Pet Duke

I have a pet dog and his name is Duke,
He is black and white and super cute.
He barks a lot at people passing by,
But all he really wants is to say 'hi'.

He likes to play football
And swim in the sea,
He always has the best fun with me.
Duke lies in the garden soaking up the sun,
When he goes for walkies
He has a crazy run.

I love my dog Duke, he really is the best,
He sleeps in my room, just to have a rest.
He gives me hugs when I am feeling sad,
He's the best dog a boy could ever have.

Connor Ditcham (7)
Sidegate Primary School, Ipswich

The Portuguese Man O' War

I glide gracefully across the open oceans.
My vibrant colours are stunning like a rainbow...
blues, pinks and purples.
I am a colossal size.
With a body shaped like a sail,
the wind softly drifts me along.
My tangling tentacles trailing behind
but beware, if you cross my path
you will get a shocking sting
like a blistering, burning blade.
I don't mean to harm you,
I'm actually nice and kind
but best to keep your distance
and stay out of my way!

Aiden Hughes (7)
Sidegate Primary School, Ipswich

My Cat!

My cat smells like flowers.
My cat's name is Matt.
My cat looks fluffy and furry.
My cat eats fish from deep in the ocean.
My cat quietly and cunningly purrs
In the middle of the night.
My cat feels soft like a hairy coat.
My cat is proud because he listens.
My cat is happy that he has me to look after him.
My cat is sensible because he wants to show other cats how to behave.

Amber Kaur Birak (7)
Sidegate Primary School, Ipswich

The Fire-Breathing Dragon

My flames are as burning as red, yellow,
swirling lava as I stomp my enormous feet
on the earthy ground.
The earth moves and the grey,
black and white rock starts bouncing
up and down.
Vicious dragons have sharp,
white teeth to bite on their meat.
They have red, deadly eyes
to scare people away.
An angry face that people do not like.
Giant ears to hear from far away.

Ananya Pravin Desai (7)
Sidegate Primary School, Ipswich

A Frog Sat On A Log

A frog sat on a log,
A frog sat on a log
And he croaked for the rest of the day.
A bee sat on a tree,
A bee sat on a tree,
Buzz, buzz, a-buzz, buzz, buzz!
He went along, stinging people
For the rest of the day.
A bull sat on a stool,
A bull sat on a stool.
Moo, moo, a-moo, moo, moo!
He kept mooing for the rest of the day.

Freddie Moy (7)
Sidegate Primary School, Ipswich

Percy The Penguin Came To School

One day, I was walking to school,
And the weather was very cool.
I opened my bag and Percy popped out
And when he popped out
He looked all about.
The first lesson was maths so I was glad
But Percy wasn't very good, so he was sad.
He wasn't any better at the rest,
But the last lesson was swimming
And he was the best.

Darcey Oakes (7)
Sidegate Primary School, Ipswich

The Peregrine Falcon

The peregrine falcon is rare indeed.
He's famous for his diving speed.
With a short tail and long pointed wings,
He glides across the countryside hunting things!
A raptor with talons, a bird of prey,
A creature of beauty, so we say.
Protect the species or before too long
We'll look around and they'll all be gone!

Lewis Rowland (7)
Sidegate Primary School, Ipswich

The Cow

Once upon a time
There was a man with a cow.
He wanted to sell the cow.
A boy wanted to buy the cow
But the man wanted a lot of money.
The boy had fifty pounds
But the man wanted a hundred pounds.
The boy gave him fifty pounds
And some magic beans to take home.
The cow's meal was delicious.

Attila Tanase (6)
Sidegate Primary School, Ipswich

Butterfly Poem

Butterfly, butterfly, beautiful butterfly with stripy wings.
Some butterflies are lazy
and some are crazy.
Some are pink, some are blue.
Some like to come out when the sun
is shining.
Some like to come out when the moon
is out.
Butterflies fly from flower to flower
and like nectar sweet.

Madelyn Ashford (7)
Sidegate Primary School, Ipswich

Rosy Rabbit

There once was a rabbit called Rosy,
Who was incredibly dozy.
She hopped into school
And fell in the pool!
When she got dry she was cosy.

Rosy's magpie friend was called Molly,
She always forgot her brolly.
When she got damp,
She made a camp
And cuddled her purple dolly.

Layla Moreno-Roberts (7)
Sidegate Primary School, Ipswich

Why Elephants Are Amazing

Elephants are big
Elephants are grey
They love to eat lots of hay.
They have families big and small
They share and care most of all
Sharing and caring is what they do
But they don't like being stuck in a zoo.
Elephants big and small
Are brave and strong
Don't forget most of all.

Reyah Amber Haayat (7)
Sidegate Primary School, Ipswich

My Friend Is A Bunny

My friend is a bunny
And is as sweet as honey.
My friend is a bunny
And jumps around happily.
My friend is a bunny
And looks so tiny.
My friend is a bunny
And it's so funny.
You think my bunny
Is funny and sunny
And if my bunny hears you shriek
It will make her leap.

Amalia Tutu (7)
Sidegate Primary School, Ipswich

Deadly Knight

The deadly knight can run around in mist.
He's very fast and can jump high
And he is not nice or happy.
He also can catch cheetahs.
He can run faster than a cheetah
But he's very strange and deadly.
He can shoot lasers too!
Also he can send out lasers
And can make submarines!

Eban Bird (7)
Sidegate Primary School, Ipswich

Crystal The Mermaid Unicorn

Crystal is a rare unicorn.
Her mummy has said she is special
since the day she was born.
She has long mermaid hair
with bright blue eyes.
So if you see Crystal the mermaid unicorn,
please can you wave and smile
as making new friends
humans or animals
is definitely her style.

Lacey Mae Wedlow (6)
Sidegate Primary School, Ipswich

The Roaring Tiger

The stripy, loud and furry tiger is orange
and it eats meat.
It lives in the jungle and it runs.
It's got razor-sharp teeth.
It's got colossal, sharp claws.
It's got a screaming good roar
and it's got super soft fur.
It's my favourite animal - the roaring tiger!

Lexi Thaine (7)
Sidegate Primary School, Ipswich

Our Cat George

Her name was George,
She was my cat.
She was skinny and not at all fat.
She would hide in the day
And go out at night
To escape our dog, Dave
Who wanted to give her a bite!
She was old and tired
And went to the vet's.
Now she's in Heaven
With all the pets.

Joseph Freezer (7)
Sidegate Primary School, Ipswich

Snappy Snake!

One sunny morning in the cold forest
there was a snappy snake
in that amazing world.
Snappy Snake slithered
through the long, green grass.
When Snappy got to the end
of the swaying grass
there was a pond.
In the amazing pond
there were hundreds of tiny, colourful fish.

Scarlett Burrows (7)
Sidegate Primary School, Ipswich

The Sly Fox

Roaming the woods, the fox hunts.
He is cunning and sly as he quietly creeps.
His prey unaware of his presence.
He feasts before climbing the hills,
The cool breeze brushing through his soft fur.
With a full belly and a smile on his face
He slowly makes his way back to the den.

Olivia Ferjani (7)
Sidegate Primary School, Ipswich

My Rabbit

I want a rabbit that's fluffy and white
so every day I can cuddle it tight.
I will call it Jessie and let it run free.
It will live in my room
and sleep next to me.
So I will ask Mummy
or if not, my dad.
If they say yes,
it will be the best present I've had!

Jessica Danielle Riley (7)
Sidegate Primary School, Ipswich

A Cheetah's Life

The cheetah runs fast
Through the savannah
Looking for food to eat.
He is joined by his sister cheetah,
Called Anna
And they run with big giant leaps.
They are fierce and spotty
And like to eat meat.
They accelerate faster than a car
And are hard to beat.

Bethany Bugg (7)
Sidegate Primary School, Ipswich

The Elephant

I am an elephant, big as can be,
My long trunk is longer than you.
I flap my ears to keep myself cool,
I am the biggest animal.
If you see me I am smart enough
To recognise myself in the mirror.
My tusks are nearly as big as your hand.
My eyes are small and round.

Zuzanna Parcinska (7)
Sidegate Primary School, Ipswich

Mr Earwig

The tree is close by
And the clouds are in the sky,
Mr Earwig crawls from under his leaf.
Its incredible teeth bite hard.
He glows in the dark.
When it's the morning it sparkles.
Mr Earwig is so much fun,
I like to find him in the sun.

Riley Emberson (7)
Sidegate Primary School, Ipswich

Guinea Pig Mysteries

Guinea pig, guinea pig, where are you?
Are you there, eating some pear?
Are you curled up in your nest asleep?
Do you dream and can you count sheep?
Come out, come out from your cage,
Bounce up and down and say hooray.

Miles William O'Keefe (7)
Sidegate Primary School, Ipswich

Cutie Panda

In the jungle lives a panda.
Sweet dreams baby panda.
You are so cuddly and so soft.
I love animals so much.
Pandas, monkeys, fish, owls and snakes.
My lovely panda friend is the best.
She is always with me.

Autumn Lily Oakes (7)
Sidegate Primary School, Ipswich

House By The River

He is tall, cute and very, very happy.
He loves to tell lots of jokes,
not just one or two.
He makes delicious and scrumptious cakes
in his house by the river.
His best friend is his teddy
called Tiger.

Yasmin Fermor (6)
Sidegate Primary School, Ipswich

The Chilli, Chilli Poem

My dog, Chilli is very silly.
She is really crazy and can be lazy.
Her tail is wiggly.
She likes her food like a piggy.
She runs very fast, she never comes last.
I love Chilli, she is my silly billy.

Bailey Miller (6)
Sidegate Primary School, Ipswich

The Sleepy Lion

Jalims the lion sleeps all day long.
He doesn't know what to do the next day.
But then he hears a deer
munching on lovely green grass.
He catches the deer
and then goes back to sleep.

Arthur Barnes (7)
Sidegate Primary School, Ipswich

Lion

Lions have big fluffy manes,
Like clouds.
Lions are scary like dragons.
Lions are loud like tigers.
Lions have big teeth
Just like hippos.

Phoebe-Mae Garrard (7)
Sidegate Primary School, Ipswich

My Giraffe

My giraffe is a clever giraffe.
He is very tall and strong.
He walks through trees
Looking for food
But my giraffe likes to laugh.

Grace Markham (7)
Sidegate Primary School, Ipswich

The Speedy Cheetah

Cheetah, cheetah, with lots of dots,
When it runs, it's hard to spot.
Cheetah, cheetah, loves to eat,
Lots of lovely juicy meat.

Rieshy Mahadevan Ramesh (7)
Sidegate Primary School, Ipswich

The Lion

The lion runs quickly.
He goes out to hunt.
He likes to run.
He climbs trees like me.
Then he jumps down and goes to sleep.
The lion has a big mane.
He is orange and his tail is long.
His teeth and claws are sharp.
The lion has little ears.

Yury Vieira (6)
St George's Primary & Nursery School, Great Yarmouth

The Horror Penguin

He eats fish.
He can swim.
He creeps up on fish then attacks.
He makes a splash and everything is OK.
He's as white as a feather
with a little bit of black on his sides.

Philip James Edwards (7)
St George's Primary & Nursery School, Great Yarmouth

The Nice Cow

The cow is black and white
with strange spots.
The cow has milk under his tummy.
He eats grass and tomatoes.
The cow moves slowly
and lays down all day.

Cory Cook (6)
St George's Primary & Nursery School, Great Yarmouth

The Golden Fish

The golden fish lives in the sea.
She is orange like the sun and moves slowly.
The fish likes swimming in the sea.
She is happy and safe in the sea.

Matas Gelumbeckas (7)
St George's Primary & Nursery School, Great Yarmouth

Elephant

Behind the big, colourful mountain
a tiny, wrinkly elephant
stretches itself like a hairband.
It has wrinkly skin like an old woman.
As loud as a trumpet, trumpety trumpet.
It never forgets.

Ellicia Soglo (6)
St John's Community Primary School & Nursery, Hoveton

Snake

Between the green, long grass
and beside a big skinny tree,
a sticky, slimy snake hides like a spider.
It strikes as fast as a cheetah.
Attacks like a vampire.
Keeps hissing like a kettle.

Mia Coxall (6)
St John's Community Primary School & Nursery, Hoveton

Lion

Below a towering tree
was a loud, fierce, great, golden cat.
It roared along the savannah.
A creeping lion with crusher jaws is off,
silently stalking like a hunter.

Hunter Lucas (5)
St John's Community Primary School & Nursery, Hoveton

Snake

On the stinky green log
a slimy, spotty snake was sleeping
like a cuddly kitten.
Strikes as fast as a cheetah.
Attacks like a bully.
Every day it goes hunting.

Barnaby Hurren (6)
St John's Community Primary School & Nursery, Hoveton

A Dragon's Aspirations

I'm content being a dragon,
Watching children live their lives.
Villagers cherish my love,
My mind forever strives.

Daniel Milton (11)
St Joseph's Catholic Primary School, Derby

Tiger, Tiger

Tiger, tiger, you are so fierce.
Tiger, tiger, I love you.
Tiger, tiger, you are so stripy.
Tiger, tiger, I love you.
Tiger, tiger, with your long thin tail.
Tiger, tiger, I love you.
Tiger, tiger, with your big black paws.
Tiger, tiger, I love you.
Tiger, tiger, with your sharp white teeth.
Tiger, tiger, I love you.
Tiger, tiger, with your wide sparkly eyes.
Tiger, tiger, I love you.
Tiger, tiger, you are so beautiful.
Tiger, tiger, I love you!

Issey Breeze
St Oswald's CE Primary School, Ashbourne

Terry The Turtle

Terry the turtle wished he was purple,
but would his wish come true?
He went to visit Wish Spider
Who lived under a wish rock,
but the wish spider said
he could only turn him blue.
So Terry the turtle sat and cried
then an orange lizard, a stripy zebra
and a colourful parrot sat down by his side.
They said, 'Be green not purple,
you're our friend, Terry the turtle.'

Sebastian Tinsley (6)
St Oswald's CE Primary School, Ashbourne

The Life Of A Leopard

First they hunt for their prey
and climb trees to stop other predators
from stealing their prey.
After eating, it's nap time.
After nap time leopards lick themselves,
to them it is a bath.
So then it's time to fall asleep again,
goodnight.
After about 12 hours, it's good morning
then they will start hunting for breakfast.

Maisie Kerr (7)
St Oswald's CE Primary School, Ashbourne

Ladybirds

Listen for ladybirds
which are flying in the air
as gentle as a feather.
And look out for the spotty, dotty insect.
Did you see it?
Yes! I've tried to catch it
but it flew away charmingly.
It hid under a plant beautifully red like Mars
with black freckles.
Delicate as a white flower petal.
Smooth as a cosy blanket.

Franek Lasek (6)
St Oswald's CE Primary School, Ashbourne

Panda, Panda, Panda, What Do You Do?

Panda, panda, panda
You climb to the tree top
Panda, panda, panda
You eat bamboo until you pop!

Panda, panda, panda
You are white and black
Panda, panda, panda
You live in a panda pack.

Panda, panda, panda
You are so soft to touch
Panda, panda, panda
I love you so very much!

Jess Wilson (7)
St Oswald's CE Primary School, Ashbourne

The Leopard

My home is in a tree.
What animal could I be?
My body is covered in roses
Which are circles just like posies.
I'm super-duper fast
As I run along the grass.
My body is elegant and athletic.
I can camouflage in the tall, yellow grass.
My body is made for speed.
I like to run and be freed!

Noah Wood (7)
St Oswald's CE Primary School, Ashbourne

Something's Stripy In The Jungle

There's something stripy in the bushes.
What it's doing nobody knows.
Is it a zebra, is it a skunk?
No, it's a scary, hairy tiger,
'Argh! Run everyone, run, run!'

Josie Leslie (7)
St Oswald's CE Primary School, Ashbourne

Monkeys

Monkeys are cheeky,
Monkeys are small,
Monkeys don't understand very much at all.
So they are cheeky!
They are also cute
And my little monkey can even play a flute!

Macy Grocott (7)
St Oswald's CE Primary School, Ashbourne

What Am I?

I am big like a tree.
I am hard like a snake.
I have flappy ears like wings.
I have a tail as long as a giraffe's tail.
I have long legs like a giraffe's legs.
I like squirting water at my friends from my trunk.
I have tusks as white as a cloud.
What am I?
An elephant.

Laura Tozer (6)
Stanground St John's Academy, Stanground

What Am I?

I am as scaly as a lizard.
I feel excited when you get me out
and play with me.
I look slimy when I slither along the ground.
I can rattle like a maraca.
I can hiss like a lizard.
I like to eat mice.
I live in a jungle.

What am I?
A snake.

Evie Rose Peacock (6)
Stanground St John's Academy, Stanground

What Am I?

I am as small as a mouse.
I feel spiky if you touch me.
I look dead if I am far away in the grass.
I sound snuffly when I move.
I can roll into a ball.
I like to eat slugs.
I am black on top and peach on the bottom.
I am a hedgehog.

Joáo Davi Gutierrez Da Silva (5)
Stanground St John's Academy, Stanground

What Am I?

I am as soft as a parrot.
I like to live in a family.
I can play like a rabbit.
I have pointy ears like a triangle.
My paws are like pillows.
I feel happy.
I purr when you stroke me.
What am I?
I am a cat.

Laura Majcher (6)
Stanground St John's Academy, Stanground

What Am I?

I am as soft as a teddy bear.
I feel fluffy as a dog.
I look as cute as a chick.
I sound happy when I purr.
I can chase a mouse.
I like to play with a ball of string.
What am I?
A cat.

Laylah Jayne Louise Jago (6)
Stanground St John's Academy, Stanground

What Am I?

I am sharp like a spiky bush.
I eat a lot of food like a squirrel.
I am as round as an orange.
I have sharp claws like a knife.
I have prickles as brown as mud.
What am I?
A *hedgehog.*

Tia Fitzpatrick (7)
Stanground St John's Academy, Stanground

What Am I?

I am as cheeky as a cheetah.
I feel as soft as a cat.
I have long arms to climb trees.
I like bananas.
I am as brown as an owl.
I like to play with my friends.
What am I?
I am a monkey.

Cherry Rae Coy (6)
Stanground St John's Academy, Stanground

What Am I?

I am as small as a hedgehog.
I feel scaly like a snake.
I look like a chameleon.
I sound quiet.
I can climb a tree one day.
I like to sit in the sun.
What am I?
A lizard.

Jaiden Walton (6)
Stanground St John's Academy, Stanground

What Am I?

I am as slithery as a lizard.
I feel scaly as a chameleon.
I look dangerous as a cheetah.
I make a hissy sound.
I can slither up a tree.
I like to slither in the grass.
What am I?

Victor D Ju (6)
Stanground St John's Academy, Stanground

What Am I?

I am as soft as a pillow.
I sound squeaky.
I feel warm and cuddly.
I look soft and cute.
I can bark.
I like staying in bed sleeping.
What am I?
I am a puppy.

Kacey Wharton (6)
Stanground St John's Academy, Stanground

What Am I?

I am as scaly as a lizard.
I feel slithery and slidy.
I look like a branch.
I sound like a cat when I hiss.
I can slither in the grass.
I like to eat leaves.

Ben Dale McBean (5)
Stanground St John's Academy, Stanground

What Am I?

I am as small as a teddy bear.
I feel furry and soft.
I am happy when I am stroked.
I can purr.
I like people tickling my tummy.
What am I?
I am a cat.

Nancy Tasker (6)
Stanground St John's Academy, Stanground

What Am I?

I am as spiky as a thorn.
I like to eat bugs.
I am as brown as dirt.
I can turn into a ball.
I only come out at night.
What am I?
I am a hedgehog.

James Owen Ady Lanning (6)
Stanground St John's Academy, Stanground

What Am I?

I like to drink milk.
I am cute.
I have four legs.
I am as soft as a teddy.
I like to play with a ball of string.
I like to eat fish.
What am I?

Aleksandra Detka (6)
Stanground St John's Academy, Stanground

What Am I?

I am soft like a carpet.
My tail is curly.
My whiskers are thin and long.
I am soft like a teddy.
I like drinking milk
What am I?
I am a cat.

Tyler Maughan (6)
Stanground St John's Academy, Stanground

I Saw A Dragon

I saw a dragon,
A dragon in the air,
Faster than a brown bear
And slower than a hare.
He's bad,
Roar, roar!
I saw a dragon,
A dragon in the lake,
Bigger than a rocket
And stronger than a locket.
Fire, fire, fire!

Anya Rai Rendle (7)
Ten Mile Bank Riverside Academy, Ten Mile Bank

Dragon, Dragon, Go Away

Dragon, dragon, go away,
run to your cave.
A dragon attacking the village.
Go away or brave St George
will kill you.
Over the castle,
fly away,
naughty, terrifying dragon.

Tianna Louise Brassett (6)
Ten Mile Bank Riverside Academy, Ten Mile Bank

Chomp, Chomp

Chomp, chomp,
going through the mountains.
What can I see?
A dragon with scary claws,
terrifying teeth and scaly wings.
He's breathing fire,
so run away.

Caroline Amanda Rolph (6)
Ten Mile Bank Riverside Academy, Ten Mile Bank

Dragon, Dragon, Dragon

Dragon, dragon, dragon,
Green, funny wings,
Skinny, rough tail.
Dragon, dragon, dragon,
Pointy, knife-like teeth,
Spiky, bumpy body.

Ella Mae Brassett (7)
Ten Mile Bank Riverside Academy, Ten Mile Bank

Dragons Usually Hide In Swamps

Dragons usually hide in swamps.
Scary and frightening.
Dragons' mouths are black or green.
Dragons have fiery breath.

Annabelle Coogan (6)
Ten Mile Bank Riverside Academy, Ten Mile Bank

Dragon, Dragon

Dragon, dragon
You can fly high
Stomp, stomp, stomp!
I hate dragons
They kill.

Angel Langley (7)
Ten Mile Bank Riverside Academy, Ten Mile Bank

What Is It?

It's as scary as a thunderstorm.
It's as furry as a dog.
It's as yellow as the sun.
Its tail is as long as my arm.
Its whiskers are as long as a shoelace.
It's as heavy as a car.
It's as loud as a crane.
Its hair is as black as coal.
It's a lion.

Grace Hills (7)
The Gainsborough Parish Church Primary School, Gainsborough

What Am I?

I have teeth like sharp blades.
My tail is long and pointy.
My favourite food is juicy meat.
I have a body bigger than an elephant.
I'm angrier than a crane.
My toenails are sharper than skewers.
I have arms longer than a meerkat.
I am a T-rex.

William Thompson (7)
The Gainsborough Parish Church Primary School, Gainsborough

What Is It?

It's as jumpy as a flamingo.
It's funny like a polar bear.
It's as cute as a dolphin.
It's as brown as a sheep.
It climbs like a leopard.
It's as cheeky as a lion.
It's as bad as a gorilla.
It's a monkey!

Holly-Anne Marie Bew (7)
The Gainsborough Parish Church Primary School, Gainsborough

What Is It?

It's as scary as a crocodile.
It's as green as grass.
Its feet are as slippery as a horn.
It's as big as a box.
It's as long as a snake.
It's as cold as ice.
It swims like a fish.
It's a Komodo dragon.

Lukus Hurst (6)
The Gainsborough Parish Church Primary School, Gainsborough

What Is It?

It's as fast as a racing car.
It's as long as a bus.
It's as scary as a thunderstorm.
It's as colourful as a rainbow.
It's as shiny as my school shoes.
Its eyes are small and angry like fire.
It's a snake.

Mylee Tuplin (6)
The Gainsborough Parish Church Primary School, Gainsborough

What Is It?

It's fatter than a meerkat.
It's heavier than a person.
It's grey like a stone.
It has a nice feeling.
It likes eating juicy fruit.
They like people.
Its ears are bigger than a mouse.
It's an elephant.

Harry Snell (6)
The Gainsborough Parish Church Primary School, Gainsborough

What Is It?

Its wings are massive like a giant.
Its arms are small like a rubber.
Its brain is like a bear.
It's big and smooth like a jumper.
It's bigger than a dog.
It's scarier than The Joker.
It is a scary pterodactyl.

Finley Thorold (7)
The Gainsborough Parish Church Primary School, Gainsborough

What Is It?

Its stripes are as black as soil.
Its long whiskers are like wire.
It's as fierce as a thunderstorm.
It eats other animals.
It's as orange as a flower.
It fights like a WWE.
It's a tiger.

Scarlett Louise Duffield (6)
The Gainsborough Parish Church Primary School, Gainsborough

What Is It?

It is as fluffy as a teddy bear.
It is as small as a ferret.
Its ears are as big as a pencil.
It's as kind as me.
It's as white as snow.
It's as soft as a dress.
It's a rabbit.

Emily Louise Ashby (6)
The Gainsborough Parish Church Primary School, Gainsborough

What Is It?

It's as scary as a lion.
It's black and red like a ladybird.
It's as mean as a leopard.
It likes dark places
And it lives in a cave.
It drinks blood.
It's a vampire dog!

Taya Beckett (7)
The Gainsborough Parish Church Primary School, Gainsborough

Mia's Riddle

It's as boring as a grumpy giant.
It's as mean as a crocodile.
It's as silly as a monkey.
It's as white as a polar bear.
It's as spotty as a leopard.
It's a dog!

Mia Rose Purvis (6)
The Gainsborough Parish Church Primary School, Gainsborough

What Is It?

It's as grey as clay.
It's as heavy as a car.
It's fatter than a rabbit.
It eats like a chomper toy.
It lives in a hot place.
It walks around a lot.
It is an elephant.

Elliot Taylor (7)
The Gainsborough Parish Church Primary School, Gainsborough

What Is It?

It's as little as a bush.
It's as cuddly as a kitten.
It's as cute as a puppy.
It's as fluffy as a pillow.
It's as jumpy as a bouncy ball.
It's a bunny rabbit!

Fern Jefferson (7)
The Gainsborough Parish Church Primary School, Gainsborough

What Is It?

It's as cute as a puppy.
It's as small as a mouse.
It's as awesome as a tiger.
It eats ice cream all day.
It lives in England.
It looks like a gremlin.
It is Stitch!

Henry Corfield (7)
The Gainsborough Parish Church Primary School, Gainsborough

What Is It?

It's as tall as a skyscraper.
It has spots like chicken pox.
It's as yellow as the sun.
It's as pretty as a sunset.
It's as happy as me.
It's a giraffe.

Yasmin Joy Clarkson (7)
The Gainsborough Parish Church Primary School, Gainsborough

What Is It?

It's as yellow as sand.
It's like a skyscraper.
It's playful like children.
It's happier than a mouse.
It's as spotty as chicken pox.
It is a giraffe.

Brooke Chapman (7)
The Gainsborough Parish Church Primary School, Gainsborough

What Is It?

It's as fluffy as a teddy bear.
It's as graceful as a butterfly.
It's bigger than a bird.
It's as brown as smoke.
Its eyes glow in the night.
It is a cat.

Ryan John Anderson (6)
The Gainsborough Parish Church Primary School, Gainsborough

It Is A Cat

It's as fluffy as a teddy bear.
It's as graceful as a butterfly.
It's bigger than a bird.
It's as white as snow.
Its eyes glow at night.
It is a cat.

Blake Palmer (6)
The Gainsborough Parish Church Primary School, Gainsborough

What Am I?

I am as woolly as a woolly mammoth.
I am as cuddly as a teddy.
I am as soft as a bed.
I eat human beings.
I live on mountains.
I sleep in the day.
I am a yeti.

Levi Coombe (7)
The Gainsborough Parish Church Primary School, Gainsborough

What Is It?

It's as cute as a cat.
It's as funny as my fish.
It's as sleepy as a lion.
It's as good as a fish.
It's as beautiful as a queen.
It's a fox!

Tayla-Mae Gray (6)
The Gainsborough Parish Church Primary School, Gainsborough

It's Callisto!

He is as soft as luxury.
He's as silly as clowns.
He is as cute as bunnies.
He loves adventuring.
His favourite food is chicken.
It's my cat, Callisto!

Maisie Pulford (7)
The Gainsborough Parish Church Primary School, Gainsborough

What Am I?

I am as brown as a puddle of mud.
I am as hairy as a cat.
I am as fun as a clown.
I eat delicious apples.
I live in a stable.
I say neigh.
I am a horse.

Amber Currie (6)
The Gainsborough Parish Church Primary School, Gainsborough

What Am I?

I am as deadly as a knife.
I am as colourful as a rainbow.
I am as spiky as a hedgehog.
I eat meat.
I live in a volcano.
I am a dragon!

Finley Wilson (7)
The Gainsborough Parish Church Primary School, Gainsborough

What Is It?

Its skin is like the sunshine.
It's as happy as a teddy bear.
Its neck is as tall as a tree.
It's as kind as me.
It's a giraffe.

Erica Fairless (6)
The Gainsborough Parish Church Primary School, Gainsborough

What Is It?

Its neck is as tall as a tree trunk.
It's as spotty as a leopard.
It's as big as an elephant.
It fights like WWE.
It is a giraffe!

Katie Rose Birkitt (7)
The Gainsborough Parish Church Primary School, Gainsborough

What Is It?

It's as fast as a car.
It's as spotty as a leopard.
It's as fierce as a lion.
It's as big as a tiger.
It's a cheetah.

Reuben Cave (6)
The Gainsborough Parish Church Primary School, Gainsborough

What Is It?

It's as yellow as sand.
Its neck is as tall as a tree.
Its ears are as big as a man.
Its spots are like chicken pox.
It is a giraffe.

Sophie Burnett (6)
The Gainsborough Parish Church Primary School, Gainsborough

Animal Friends

It is as fluffy as a fluff ball.
It is as soft as a pillow.
It is as soft as a baby.
It is as loving as a dog.
It is a cat called Milly!

Amber Brewer (7)
The Gainsborough Parish Church Primary School, Gainsborough

Maddison's Riddle

It's as spotty as a giraffe.
It's as funny as a leopard falling off a tree.
It's faster than a speeding car.
It is a cheetah.

Maddison Merrills (6)
The Gainsborough Parish Church Primary School, Gainsborough

What Am I?

I'm as stripy as a zebra.
I'm as fierce as a lion.
I'm as silly as a monkey.
I eat meat.
I growl.
I am a tiger!

Keela Galloway (7)
The Gainsborough Parish Church Primary School, Gainsborough

Logan's Riddle

It's as grey as a dull rain cloud.
It's as ginormous as a giant.
Its trunk is as squirty as a water gun.
It is an elephant.

Logan Dre Woodrow (6)
The Gainsborough Parish Church Primary School, Gainsborough

What Is The Animal?

It's as cute as a budgie.
It's very fluffy like a fluff ball.
It's as funny as a monkey.
It's a dog called Paddy!

Freya Mawer (7)
The Gainsborough Parish Church Primary School, Gainsborough

The Elephant

It's as dull as a rain cloud.
It's as ginormous as a giant.
Its trunk is as squirty as a water gun.
It is an elephant.

Joel Waller (5)
The Gainsborough Parish Church Primary School,
Gainsborough

What Is It?

It's as cheeky as a monkey.
It's as fluffy as a bunny.
It's as adorable as a baby.

It is a cat!

Laura Moutinho (7)
The Gainsborough Parish Church Primary School, Gainsborough

What Is It? Guess!

It's as glittery as a picture.
It's as fluffy as a fluff ball.
It can fly higher than a cloud.
It's a unicorn!

Ellie Drayton (6)
The Gainsborough Parish Church Primary School, Gainsborough

What Is It?

It is as scaly as a snake.
It is as creepy as a lion.
It is as fast as a tiger.
It is a python.
How amazing is that?

Tobey Hallam (6)
The Gainsborough Parish Church Primary School, Gainsborough

What Is My Animal?

It's as quiet as a rabbit.
It's as grey as an elephant.
It's as lonely as a snake.
It's a koala bear.

Kristie Denniss (7)
The Gainsborough Parish Church Primary School, Gainsborough

What Is It?

It's as cuddly as a teddy.
Its nose is as little as a button.
It's as graceful as a butterfly.
It is a cat.

Courtney Anna Gloria Turner (6)
The Gainsborough Parish Church Primary School, Gainsborough

What Am I?

I am as fierce as a tiger.
I am as soft as a pillow.
I am as scary as a ghost.
I eat meat.
I am a lion!

Harry James Townsend (7)
The Gainsborough Parish Church Primary School, Gainsborough

What Is It?

It's as cute as a lion.
It's as playful as a kangaroo.
It's as scary as a clown.
It is a cat.

Kacie-Jo White (6)
The Gainsborough Parish Church Primary School, Gainsborough

What Is It?

It is as happy as a monkey.
It is as silly as a clown.
It is as white as ice.
It is a polar bear.

Leah Potts (5)
The Gainsborough Parish Church Primary School, Gainsborough

What Is It?

It's as tough as a rock.
It's as strong as an ox.
It's as big as a bus.
It's a rhino!

Liam Levick (7)
The Gainsborough Parish Church Primary School, Gainsborough

What Am I?

I am big.
I am cute.
I am fierce.
I am furry.
I eat meat.
I roar.
I am a lion!

Maisie Grace Swinton (6)
The Gainsborough Parish Church Primary School, Gainsborough

What Am I?

I am hard to break.
I am small.
I am as disgusting as ear wax.
I am a millipede.

Maximiliaan Kwant (6)
The Gainsborough Parish Church Primary School, Gainsborough

What Am I?

I have a furry mane.
I am crazy.
I eat meat.
I am sleepy.
I am a lion.

Corey Simons (6)
The Gainsborough Parish Church Primary School, Gainsborough

What Is It?

It is long.
It is wriggly.
It will scare you.
It is a snake!

Oonagh Stark (6)
The Gainsborough Parish Church Primary School, Gainsborough

What Is It?

It is tall.
It is long-necked
It is big
It is a giraffe.

Hanna Corringham (5)
The Gainsborough Parish Church Primary School, Gainsborough

What Is It?

It is cheeky.
It is bad.
It is naughty.
It is a monkey.

Declan McConnell (6)
The Gainsborough Parish Church Primary School, Gainsborough

What Is It?

I am slimy.
I am sleepy.
I am funny.
I am a tortoise.

Alex Jennings (5)
The Gainsborough Parish Church Primary School, Gainsborough

What Is It?

It is slimy.
It is noisy.
It is scary.
It is a snake.

Noah Stobbs (6)
The Gainsborough Parish Church Primary School, Gainsborough

What Is It?

It is furry.
It is cute.
It is fluffy.
It is a cat.

Phoebe-Louise Garnham (6)
The Gainsborough Parish Church Primary School, Gainsborough

Animal Homes

Some animals live in homes
But only if you adopt them.
You have got to take good care of your pet.
You have to feed them dog food
And tap water.
Let your dog in the garden.
You've got to take your pets on a long walk
Only if you are not at work.
If you are at work
Take your pet for a short walk.
If you're allergic to animals,
Don't get an animal.
If you love animals get one,
Only if you are not allergic to animals.
So take good care of your pets.
If it is a dog or a cat,
Take them for walks,
Feed them and let them out

In the garden for a week.
If you don't your house will stink!

Layla Kerry Smith (7)
Westhouses Primary School, Westhouses

The Day Out

One day there was a dude called Harry.
He liked boats and other rides.
So he jumped on a boat.
And then he went on an aeroplane to Spain.
Then he went on a bus to the zoo.
He looked at the snakes,
Then he went to look at the chickens.
Then he went in a taxi back home
To get a chocolate ice cream,
And went to a party.
'It was fun!' Harry said.

Liam Lowe (7)
Westhouses Primary School, Westhouses

Cheeky Monkey

Cheeky monkey,
His name is Monkey King.
He's very cheeky, he's dark brown.
He does a triple backflip,
He's super ugly.
He lives in a dark forest.
He eats green bananas.
He swings very fast.
He throws dirty banana skins,
He steals shiny things.
He breaks babies' toys,
He's the meanest!

Mason Greaves (6)
Westhouses Primary School, Westhouses

Rose

I have a cat called Rose,
She is dark black, bright white and soft.
She loves being stroked.
She is very cute.
I love her and she loves me.
She lives in my nice cool house.
She goes around the house
But mostly in my mum's room.
She eats cat food,
Most of all she wants to sleep!

Joseph David Morton (6)
Westhouses Primary School, Westhouses

Animals Poem

Rudy was a cute and cuddly, fast cat.
She was bright brown
And lived in a lighthouse.
She was very good at running
And jumping.

She jumped and played and ate
But what she liked most
Was sleeping in her mum's bedroom.
She did the best trick ever...
A front flip!

Emmi (7)
Westhouses Primary School, Westhouses

The Silly Seal

There was a silly, funny, cuddly
and friendly seal swimming in the sea.
He was captured, sorted
and sold to a circus.
They told them to give him to a water place
to get him cold
because he was very hot in the circus.
So he was sent to Center Parcs'
Sea Life Centre.

Olivia Wilson (6)
Westhouses Primary School, Westhouses

Exquisite Castle Cat

Princess Lai lived in an exquisite castle
And she was happy.
She was young and small,
Cute and cuddly.
She was crimson.
She liked to eat meat,
Play and sleep every day.
She was playful and cute.
She was playful and kind!

Paiton Toseland (7)
Westhouses Primary School, Westhouses

Young Writers Information

We hope you have enjoyed reading this book – and that you will continue to in the coming years.

If you're a young writer who enjoys reading and creative writing, or the parent of an enthusiastic poet or story writer, do visit our website www.youngwriters.co.uk. Here you will find free competitions, workshops and games, as well as recommended reads, a poetry glossary and our blog.

If you would like to order further copies of this book, or any of our other titles give us a call or visit www.youngwriters.co.uk.

**Young Writers, Remus House, Coltsfoot Drive, Peterborough, PE2 9BF
(01733) 890066**

info@youngwriters.co.uk